ALL US BEAUTIFUL MONSTERS

Also by Alex Lemon

Another Last Day

Feverland

The Wish Book

Fancy Beasts

Happy

Hallelujah Blackout

Mosquito

All Us Beautiful Monsters

POEMS

Alex Lemon

MILKWEED EDITIONS

milkweed.org

Published 2026 by Milkweed Editions
Printed in Canada
Cover design by Mary Austin Speaker
Cover artwork by Ralph Eugene Meatyard,
Romance (N.) from Ambrose Bierce #3, 1962

Author photo by Lawrence Jenkins
26 27 28 29 30 5 4 3 2 1
First Edition

Library of Congress Cataloging-in-Publication Data

Names: Lemon, Alex author
Title: All us beautiful monsters : poems / Alex Lemon.
Description: First edition. | Minneapolis, Minnesota : Milkweed Editions, 2026. | Summary: "A deeply imaginative sixth collection by a beloved poet who renders in loving detail the complexities of life, in all its terror and wonder"-- Provided by publisher.
Identifiers: LCCN 2025032240 (print) | LCCN 2025032241 (ebook) | ISBN 9781639551828 trade paperback | ISBN 9781639551835 ebook
Subjects: LCGFT: Poetry
Classification: LCC PS3612.E468 A76 2026 (print) | LCC PS3612.E468 (ebook)
LC record available at https://lccn.loc.gov/2025032240
LC ebook record available at https://lccn.loc.gov/2025032241

For Ariane, Felix, & Alma

Contents

FOUR

FIVE

ALL US BEAUTIFUL MONSTERS

AWKWARD HUG

There is so much
Salvageable magic

Tremoring inside
Us cow-dumb fucks,

But we turn away,
Spend our days deep

In the dark woods
Arguing with trees until

The bark swirls
With ambulance

Light. *There, there.*
I'm wide open so come

On in here. Soon, each
Morning, you will tremble,

Glow, feeling the ticking
Pulse of the new bomb

That wakes in each of us.

ONE

And in the lowest deep a lower deep
Still threat'ning to devour me

—John Milton, *Paradise Lost*

VOODOO CALISTHENICS

We play feverish tricks in the unforgiven
Light. Paradise of cobwebs. We are jagged-
Throated in the mannequin lounge

On the darksome concrete others
Call next-stop-the-cemetery. Pre-worm
Pre-face-on-a-milk-carton. Swans

Fly out of our piles of turned dirt. All
The animals come to lay eggs in our
Graves. O' fake flowers above the real

Blood. What does anyone think before
The bones burn white—those after-
Noons that couldn't have been any

Better: drawing vegetables on our nakedness
With a vanilla-scented marker & then biting
Them smeary, erased. The night wind swills—

Charred fish, the tang of burning plastic
A scurry in the gutter & what a soundtrack
The cicadas & purring streetlamps make.

This *is* the world & always it is the perfect time
To play emergency room. Hustle. Hurry
On in. Welcome back to being alive.

COZY

A little needlepoint a little
Scalding   I sing lullabies
To myself in the dark   I have

          Told this

To no one   Your exact
& beautiful so much   I promise
     To swagger into

          The next

Life   A little needlepoint a little
Scalding   I sing   Lullabies
To myself

          In the dark

All slick   Sorry
I say   Pennies hot beneath
My tongue   I've told this

          Beautiful so much

I sing lullabies   To myself
In the dark   I promise
I've told   A little needlepoint

          A little scalding & go

NO DOOR NO

Welcome
to my party
of special

favors—waiting
cages gaped
open table ablaze
with perfect

silver & molten
blitzcake the tease
heavy-breathing

sweat down your
neck howlsugar
from our night-

mare garden
O blossoming
sweet glow
O cherry bomb

THE RIGHTEOUS MAN IS AN ADVOCATE OF ALL CREATURES

Let us speak
Not of how
Much wickedness

We have within
Us, but how amazing
It is that we don't
Commit more

Stick-'em-ups.
Celebrate it, sing—
Great shamalam!

Bumpleberry
Steamabout! I have
Had numerous out

Of body experiences
With Halloween
Masks & through their
Crescented eyes,

Learned that our
Mouths are wonder
Cabinets. *Gooseneck*

Inferno! Ripple me & snort!
Let's spend our remaining

Days pretending to
Share a heart—we'll be

Conjoined sisters,
Sweating through
Our magical panties.

How breathtaking.
We are marvelous
Brides of daylight.
We taste it all.

SLOW CLOUD

A gathering bang
Spreads purple-
Lipped across dawn—

So unseam me,
Bewonder

The black forest sings

A wooden bowl spilling
Thickly over

Steam from
Our tricked-out
Holes

All low down
Like nothing sweet
Will ever touch you

Emberlight in the drooping
Shadows of live oaks

Dead deer are waking
Up all around us

FEVERISH

So many little
Revelations
In morning's waltzing

Light—Whippoorwill
Edged distinctly, luminous

An explosion of feathers
Pale electric against

The grass-dead fence line—

The instant night puckers
Fully away

The backyard whelps beautiful
Bathed in the kitchen's soily light

The hollows inside

My mouth open
For that jiggering glow

In the pecan trees outside
The wind of kissing
Time gusts

High above this mealy earth
Where we live on top of our always

Listening dead
Their forever
Asking

Are you on good terms
With what little is inside you?

TWO

I'm a man on fire walking down your street
With one guitar & two dancing feet
Only one desire that's left in me
I want the whole damn world
To come dance with me

—Edward Sharpe and the Magnetic Zeros,
"Man on Fire"

MORE BEING WONDROUS

We been doubled-over, gassed
With laughter as we cry blood
Into the dirt. We been worn out.
We been outside, looking through
The window, kicking in the door.
We been looked through like windows,
A sheet of clear plastic blown
Into traffic. We been saying good-
Bye, saying hello, how are you,
Would you like to try to break me
Into a thousand shards of light, like
The stars twirling above us, across
The stretch of wine dark in our heads,
The burning hull of our chests—folding
In on itself as the days pass, as the stars
Burst around us or are they fires
In the distance, sparks igniting tinder
In the ditches, or just the loneliest
Boy in the world juggling fire
Forever. He can't stop, he doesn't stop.
The air around him feels like velvet,
A too-tight shirt, a small box, a coffin
Ready to be lowered into the mealy
Ground, where we been digging &
Digging. We been holding it in our hands,
Rubbing it into our tongues, pocketing
It in our lips. We been like moonlight.
Like moonlight on half-smoked cigarettes,
Like moonlight on a tractor chugging
Down the street with no tractor. We

Been forgetting in the dark, waking at
Twilight. We been filled. We been empty.
We been walking & it sounds like faraway
Tambourines, one low prayer bowl, singing
Closer & closer. We been closed out & gotta
Go. We been busted up & oh so pretty, shining
In the darklight, swaying in the wolflight. We
Been seeing you all in heaven, in hell, in this place
In between what we imagine anything else might
Be. Hear it again: we been pretty, oh so pretty,
Spill-hearted, bruised by sunlight with this joy so big.
We been breaking open, pretty, oh so pretty, love-
Sheared, broke-tooth, smiling pretty & whole.

BUGS NEED HUGS

Bitch, you crazy,
The dark thickening
Elmgrove whispered.
I cried out, showed
Them that instead
Of thumbs I was
Born with rabbits'
Feet. The hundreds
Of eyes that stared
At me did not blink.
To push back against
The fear, I turned
Myself into a machine
With arms that did
Not stop chopping.
A symphony of slide
Whistles thickened
The brambling dark
With music. I ran one
Hundred miles per
Hour toward the moon-
Light, somersaulting,
Finally, into a shorn
Grass field that looked
Snow-frosted. On
My back, I lay down
In the brightness, trying
To breathe. Like steel
Wool, the glow
Scoured my face

Until my entire body
Roiled. My skin
Tugged as if it was
Tearing away from
The rest of me.
The insects on me
Glinted, churned. Thorax.
Abdomen. Every-
Where, wings. My flesh
Was the surface
Of the ocean. In their
Dice-rattling noise
I heard someone say
That soon, I would
Conquer flight. Above:
A few wayward clouds,
Enormous TVs
Flickering on & off
In each. I tried to
Find my heart by
Using the last tool
I had on me, my mind.
For the first time
I really thought about
Where that bloodbag
Might be hiding out,
But my furry thumbs
Had turned in for
The night. I pushed
Into all of my known
Soft parts with
Everything an arm-
Less man like me

Has. The tiny hope
I had for just a pitter-
Patter or burble
Flushed, flickered,
Then went black.
But around me, night
Spangled joyously.
I traced my stars—
The constellations
I tell no one about—
Gasoline Can, Man With
Hook Hand & I felt
Its pumping presence
In me. An oven.
A refinery fire. Impossible
To contain. Endless.
Silent & roaring.

MISERICORDIA

Maybe it is wonderful—

How slow every life

How every slow life

Shudders forward

Every life a slow
Motion

Mistake—
Of photographs, stills
From an ashy film—

It's hard to tell
The good things
From the bad

The masks they share
Clothes, they are

The same nostalgia

Nothing & needlefaced

I'VE GOT NO BUSINESS TO ATTEND TO

Dinosaur kale, a rusty waffle
Iron, a rustling wheeze in

The baby crib on the curb—
I don't know what to call all

Of my promises: *Beasts*
Rising from the mist-

Scarved dark or *Things could*
Be different but who knows

Where that good shit is going
Down. San Marcos, Cherry Creek,

Even high noon's bed of nails.
Over there: a field of dead

Possums—sunflowers
Growing out of each

Skull. Right here: a spilled
Slurpee sprawled into

A sidewalk Jackson Pollock.
What holds this pinwheeling

Brightness inside me when
Wind gusts through each cut,

Each of my breaks—how does
It stay when healing has no end?

OM NOM

These blistery days cloak so amazingly
Around us, don't they? This earth
That wobbles & spins, crowded
With never-ending waves of new
Mouths mewling & electromagnetic
Radiation. Here, where everyone gets
A trophy to pile atop the rest of our
We can't ever ever get enough, where
It's always happy hour somewhere
& somewhere else a manatee stares
Into the sunshine with its dead eyes
As it floats its bloated way toward
Nevermore. & everywhere in between,
Deep in the noshine, we have so much
Bloviating to do—so much to moo
About nothing at all—So, he was
Like reciting lines about the bottom
Of his heart & she was like *whatever,*
The bridge's crumbling pylons & then
This is where everyone gets up & starts
Dancing & sings the monkey mind is
Miraculous! Donkey powder & lasers
Have given us sight & scorched off
Our stretch marks! Come on! Let's play
Blackjack or better yet, make a bunch
Of babies no one knows how to raise!
But now the lights are getting dim.
The curtain swooshes shut. There's
A cough. Everyone blinks, picks barnacles
From their eyes. Titter, yawn, titter in the waiting

Dark & then the spotlight booms & a mic
Falls all the way from heaven & bounces
& flangs off the floor. *For real*, nothing says
Into the mic & that's funny, it sounds like
It's coming from the bright blank circle of light
Where an MC should be. *Listen up now, you*
Crumbsnatchers. The voice is coal hewn & deep.
Before you return to the dirt & become the gift
Of dirt—that timbre, it's got to be Robert Goulet
Or Nina Simone or who the fuck knows, Moses
Maybe?—*Each still face must be kissed & kissed*
& kissed—No, that's not it either. Because of the twang,
You think it's got to be Jimmy Dean still preaching
The gospel of link, patty, heart attack, but oh no,
Not this again, you can feel it now. The voice bucks
Against your ribs. There's a darkness inside you
Singing, hammocked in a tangle of red jellies. It jangles
The viscera something sweet, a burning tire smell—
We're all a bit rashy, inner thighs splotched with ringworm
& a skin funk that can't stop, won't stop & won't heal.
It floods back into you, that voice, the good old bandit
Inside you with its unstoppable timbre—*Dead zones*
In the oceans. Alligators biding their time
In golf course water hazards—When you were little
It chewed up Now I Lay Me Down to Sleep & spit
Back a love everwhiplashing that made you want
To wear the skin of everyone around you. See No,
Hear No, Speak No, you thought through
Your teenage years, but you could never finish
That & instead took naps in the sunshine with a
Gorilla mask on. *Sooner or later, we're all going*
To take those blazing dirt naps—monstrous & beautiful
& perfect & failing—How did you ever fool yourself that

It had been gone—*All of us watching our skin as it pulls off*
& floats away. How bright it becomes after the last thing we see—
The nostalgia twists your insides & you yearn—*All of us*
Getting better & more lovely but because it has to be,
Still just as ready to slip a screwdriver into a stranger's gut—
The lights flicker. Let it end, you plead. Let it out
Of me—*Chests opened for hammers to be thrown*
At our nail-shaped hearts. Our infinite puffs of dust.
The lights go out. *But did you see what time it is?*
Each & every one of us Grand Puba Chop Chop
Or Bro Bro Hackles. After a slip & shish inside you
It flattens out & becomes almost pleasant, a shower
Of foamed honey. It becomes so hard to sliver open
Your eyes & see absolutely no one around you.
Frayed scraps left on the swan-white bones becoming
More & more beautiful, the best kind of dirt. When
You look down a sheen of black glass has taken
The place of your legs & you're sinking slowly
Into it—*Let the world without us dip their snouts*
Into our opened bodies & slurp & tug & taste how
Bland & unsurprisingly chicken-flavored we all
Were. It's a flushed bath, this sinking. You're going.
A hot gasp & going-all-the-way red works over
The body. It is being dipped in a furnace of melted glass,
This downward letting go where somehow the self sings
Hallelujah! & *How the fuck did we let this crazy mess*
Happen? & *Good Riddance* then one final *Hallelujah!*
Right before a lowlight reel of hands opening
Click-clicks before your eyes, dropping, in slow
Motion, thing after thing into what used to be
Your lap: pomegranate seeds, a harmonica, a yank
Of felt, a feather, handfuls of pencil shavings
& then nothing at all. The hands opening over

& over again but nothing comes. Starbursts all around
You in the heavy-metal dark. It's womblike now.
Or maybe it's the stutterer's spark—what will
Always rhyme with highwiring in stormy weather.
All of the things you've done feel heavier
& heavier & though you think you're free & clear,
There's a purpling heat in the throat, gulping
Its way down & deeper. A bonfire of racing
Dominos falling into each other & then into pieces.
Just like the one that flared up in front of you
As you tried to navigate I-35's rush-hour traffic
& had to choose: back of the semi or guardrail.
Who knew that the answer to both was
Uselessness. Hands gauze-wrapped, two
Bowling ball–sized Q-tips. But all of you feels
Gorgeous in the burning inside you.
The crackling inferno's pops & tears.
Cinders tornado up from whatever you
Used to be, but there's so little left: crashing
Waves of catcalls & dinnertime whistles
& come on heartzip, get over here
Black eye & how'd that go for you. Cinders upward
Shearing, curves of blindlit scratches in the air.
You look up one last time & there's a mobile
Above you in the deep-ass dark—pearls & glowworm
Nubs & hot pepper lights & shot glasses
Filled neon orange, & beyond that, a sky
Filled with wingless seagulls & warplanes & full
Lips that whisper unhearable things. Turning,
The constellations above you turning & turning.
The song inside you almost to the end
You've never heard but know & you reach
Up, grasping for peeling light, stretched out,

Hands clawing open & closed. *What's left of us,*
What hasn't been picked & torn away
In long strips of flesh—You reach for the wayward
Brightness. Again & again. It will be thousands
Of years before you're able to press the radiance
Into the sockets of your eyes, but you don't care
Anymore. The song, you know, will go on, too—
Fading in & out & away, an everlasting
& Doppler in between emergencies
& timeout little busters. Always & forever.
Grace at the tongue tip & standing out
On the front steps, candles lit & harmonizing.

I GET COLLECT CALLS FROM THE WAY UP TOP

When I think real hard
I can understand every-
Thing—Nuclear peptides.
Hyperlipidemia. Even
The reverse goatee. Once
I thought so intensely
My neighbor doused
Himself in gasoline,
Turned into the Human
Torch in front of McDonald's
Big greasy windows. Ages
Ago, I was voted All-Time
President of the enormous fly-
Whirling mulch pile in
The backyard. The wind
Wolf whistles, whispers
That I am a dictator
But I take off my shirt
So the sky can see my toothy
Scars, the footprint-shaped
Burns that your last coup
D'état flowered over me.
I never know when you will
Arrive. The truth of it: dark
In the faraway of me I crave
It. When the decaying soil
Is mine, I am a most benevolent
Ruler—the wreck of banana
Peels & coffee grounds is well-
Maintained, massaged by these

Dexterous hands with love,
Precision & grace. There is a man
That someone seems to keep
Shackled in the basement who
Crawls outside, sings lullabies
Into the rot. I could kiss
That fool, but my vigilance
Allows no time for weakness.
Every morning there are hundreds
Of dead birds on the lawn—
Each one to be folded into silk
Panties, thrown like a grenade
Into the public pool across
The street & there, in
The deathy sweetness
That weeps from their beaks
I smell your surprise—you are
Closing in, always, on my heels,
Right behind me, nearly, sitting
On my shoulder, almost, inside me.

FALLING ASLEEP AT THE WHEEL

In the parking lot watching
The skaters & their rail-sliding
Radness I realized the grief suit
I was wearing would bum
Out all the strangers at the after-party

So I went back in time & mummied
A gunnysack around my head, snuffing
Myself out for a few days
With darkness & Tony's ether.
Next thing I know I'm careening

Through a screen door with all of that
Invulnerability thundering through
My body & then POOF—suddenly
I'm javelining lightning bolts
At moonwalking bunnies in the backyard

Of my childhood home, & POOF—
I'm in my college-squalor apartment,
Introducing myself to the downstairs neighbor,
Squid legs curtaining my face: *hello, howdy, pour*
A cup of sugar in my mouth, & POOF—

I'm waking up, mid-ruling, Chief Justice
Of the Supreme Court asking the plaintiff
To name just one motherfucker that did
Not start as a baby & then softer, almost
Unhearable—POOF—& I'm right here—

Smack dab on planet nowhere, awaiting
The infinite ways a body can absorb
Pain as night blackens—nailholes of light
Turning, turning, turning around me.

YESTERDAY'S BALLOON IS TOMORROW'S MOTORCYCLE HELMET

Eating pepitas below
The wind-trembling
Trees, I go glaze-
Eyed. If we never
Stare into the sky,
Pick out the skull-shaped
Clouds that twin
Our dead loved ones,
What kind of navel-
Gazing grace are we
Working with? What
Kind of life is one
Where, over the years,
You don't eat a few
Pounds of dirt?
A thrush hopping
Through the tree's
Peaches. Spiderwebs
Like glass. The days
Teem with these
Minor ceremonies
& breakables. Sun-
Dappled, I converse
With my ghosts,
Blushing with blood.
It is unfathomable—
The densest love,
Almost painful,
A shining block

Of concrete caverned
In my chest. Believing
Their whispers has
Gotten harder & harder—
The wind picks up,
A tumble of leafy light,
They go on & on—
We're all damned if
We do & damned if we don't.

THREE

a siren whining high toward town repeating
that the emergency is not here, repeating
that this loud silence is only where you live

—Ada Limón, "Late Summer after a Panic Attack"

PEELERS

It's always neon in
The Skinner

Box, Amateur hour
On this planet of ass-slappers

Us doomlusters
Pray to be rotten
With fish-bellied tricks

But we're dog-skulled. All heart-
Worm & bleeding

Gums. How much for
You to crawl

Inside & wear me around
Like a suit
Of armor, a summer dress
Splayed

In this cataract of darkness
Our grins glow
The slow back

RENOVATIO

When I breathe deep,
Take a good look far

Down inside myself,
I see gossiping freeways

Of blood, a slick red
Cosmos of guts

Dancing the *Special*
Delivery, Just Open

The Goddamn Door.
It feels like someone

Took the air out
Of the world if I go

Too far down. So quickly
It becomes that dream

Where I'm surrounded
By masked people working—

Snap eeek snap into
Rubber gloves.

But one time I did it. I pushed
On & the light faded

Red to blue & then
Black. I woke beneath

A sky so blue my molars
Cracked. I try so hard

Not to forget—
When everything is

Perfect, nothing is very
Good, that the fist

Of tightness I feel
In my throat is really

The bottomless joy
I have for being alive.

I could see all the inviable
Things in the world—

The wisdom of gumball
Machines & animals

That zigzag out of forest
Fires. Soon, it hurt each time

My heart thumped. Sticky
Water streamed from

My eyes, gumming slugs
Down my sleepy cheeks.

Each day folded into itself.
A man stood before me

In the shaving mirror
With a blasted-apart

Look. One day he told me
That no matter how calm,

Radiant & unstoppable I might feel,
It was too late. I'd long ago decided

To be dead. *Deodorant can't help*
Ugly, he said & suddenly there

We were—Me & the man in
Me, neck-deep in the bathtub.

Water rioting, a full boil.
As if hundreds of white-hot

Mouths were suckering
Like lampreys at my skin,

Suckling for anything
That might fill the bottomless

Black hole growing
Like triplets inside us.

PLEASE STOP TALKING LET US LISTEN

You are more likely
To be stung bloated

& dead, by a swarm
Of bees, than be killed

By a gun-toting burglar.
Fingernails grow faster

Than toenails. Every four
Days you have a new

Stomach lining. You will
Produce a swimming pool

Of saliva in your life-
Time. Eating a backpack

Of prunes each day
Will make you piss

Rainbows. Hallucinogens,
Diuretics in the gas-tasting

Tap water. The beach bristles
With glass shards & Triops.

Dig yourself that hole
With so much fervor

That you can taste the hot
Damn in the world

Firecracking around you.
Stare into the sun. Pay

Attention to what the clouds
Say. Everything begins, then

Ceases to exist before beginning
Once again. Throatsilver. Stardust.

Deadflesh. Insects are being
Born inside you & it burns.

RECESS

Once you realize
How uncertain
It is, it all becomes

Clear. Clouds—
The sky's craters.

Spit-polished skulls
Stacked in storefront
Displays. The hallmark

Of grief etched into
The air by songbirds.

Each morning
The magnolias
Ablaze with hope.

APPETITE FOR DESTRUCTION

Mark this language, my beautiful
Sinners, because the words
Coming out of my mouth are
Not mine. Oh no. Oh no!
Paradise is speaking through me
Right now & that honey sounds
Good, right? Oh, it is sweet.
So, so sweet. It's time to listen
Up. Listen to it now! Exactly
One year after the asteroid
Hits & waves of blood sweep
The streets, your Auntie Boo-
Bucket will be astraddle a bucking
Dinosaur as it bounds over the lava-
Torn land & if you do all the goody
Goody you can now, she will find
Some of you emerging from the muck,
Nurse y'all back to your fighting weights
So one of you can take your rightful place
As Lord of the Manatees. But whoa—
I must slow down! Slow down, I must
Say to myself. Slow it down! I am
Ahead of myself. So far ahead. I
Don't mean to make you uncomfortable
But until then it's night sweats,
A few lost fingers & repeated blood
Poisonings that finally, finally, finally,
Will trumpet the arrival of a beatific
Voice in some of your heads. It will sing
Happy Birthday, Mr. President & summer

Jams from your embarrassing youths. It
Will sing *How'd That Taste* & *All I Can*
Tell You About Hemophilia. It will sing—
Sing it will & it won't stop. It can't
Stop. My friends, we will be forced
Face down into manure lagoons
Until we say we love each second
Of it. This is the way it will be, my
Lovelies. We all want to know what it
All means. Right? What does the meanness,
What does your face seen in the face
Of another mean? Can't know. Want
To know. Won't know. For this, I am
Truly sorry. But before we get off
This bus, before we spend our day
Together, all of you should know:
All of us are deserving of substantial
Compensation! Hold your breath!
Listen to all the tiny lumberjacks
Inside you! You need it again? Let
Me translate it for you—Hear it all
In the glugging syrup! The pit vipers!
Beluga tongues! Rum ponders! Shit
Glum! Today, we may be beleaguered
On this bus here together, but think
Of the many tomorrows from now
That will find us blanket-covered & flea-bit
With not even one prescription painkiller
To rattle in a bottle. Close your eyes,
Think of that someone you love real
Strong right now, that someone who
Right this very moment, may or may not be,
But probably most definitely is, cooking

Meth in a camper at the state park just outside
Of Fresno. Hold on & hold me. Fresno
No more. There are softshell turtles glittering
In Faribault. So Faribault it is—Faribault
Is spackled with your love & the bigger
You love, the more Faribault shudders.
So ride on, my albino pandas! There are
Bananas in the moonlight! Bananas for
Everyone & enough for all. Remember as
You go forth—This bus won't be coming
Back—this here is the last stop for all of us.
Philadelphia or pedophilia! Rabbit pox
Or Rochester! Don't you worry about
The bedwetting. No longer fear the Rip
Bag theory. Please don't weep. Please.
If I can leave you with anything at all,
Let it be this. We are the same junkyards!
I know so little about what happens
Around us, but I can't but love
Every goddamn second of this!
So congratulations, my lumphearts,
Your trophies will arrive, they will find you.

IT IS YOUR TURN TO CARRY ME TO THE EMERGENCY ROOM

The midnight oaks
Guard the park

Like electrified
Skeletons & pretty

Much each question
That sears me sleepless

Is so huge I can't
Even begin finding

Ways to answer them.
My words go lost

In the thimbleberry.
Nothing bad is going

To happen, ever, ever.
A perfectly starless

Night curtains my
Head. *Too often the voice*

I hear inside me is that
Of a complete stranger.

A square of light
Opens & closes in

My chest—the jaw
Of a rainbow trout

Mawing, a dumpster
Lid dropped shut,

Flung wide. *It will*
Go on. It will never

Stop, never. I practice
Picking up fallen

Apples in the total
Dark, do my best

To cut just the bad
Parts away & fling

Them skyward, up
On the roof. *Already,*

I'm awash in remorse
For not having lived

Well enough. Lightning
Switchbacks, ladders

My bones. Glint,
Shine—the gutters

Shake in the wind. I do
Not want to be a man,

I want to be dynamite.
All these years & still,

I refuse to learn that
I should feel guilty for

Wanting to pound
A motherfucker to

Cherry mush. One
Of these days I know

The dirt will gape
Open right in front

Of me & out will climb
A better version

Of myself. But the bats
Tonight must be black

Doves & I think about
The growing boy & his

Mother sleeping in
There & my chest

Whips electric like
A downed power line.

The skin gloved too
Tight around me

Sizzles, hums.

ALL US BEAUTIFUL MONSTERS

The entire world wants
To be an oldster with Alzheimer's
In a big-box store, wandering
The aisles shouting, endlessly—
But I am pretty sure that today
Is my day to not just be any old
Guy but to be *the* guy. A baby grows
In each drawer of the million-
Drawered cherrywood cabinet
That is my head & to keep
This army of tender brutes warm
Before heading to the strip mall,
I put on your coonskin hat.
I swallow a fistful of stones
You stole from the Alamo.
It is like it is each time—not
Just like returning to the womb—
It is as if the womb sucked me up
Into the starlight like a spaceship.
Nothing came before us, I suppose.
Tonight, we will once again forgive
Ourselves for the people that have
All gone missing while under
Our care. Fireworks will splash
The sky with a pink wave & we
Will both jump back, feigning
To look at what we've done, exactly
In the same way. Like lobsters
Hammering missives back & forth
With claw & rock, when it goes

Black, we will bang our fists
On whatever's closest to speak
To each other about
The loveliness all over us.

FOUR

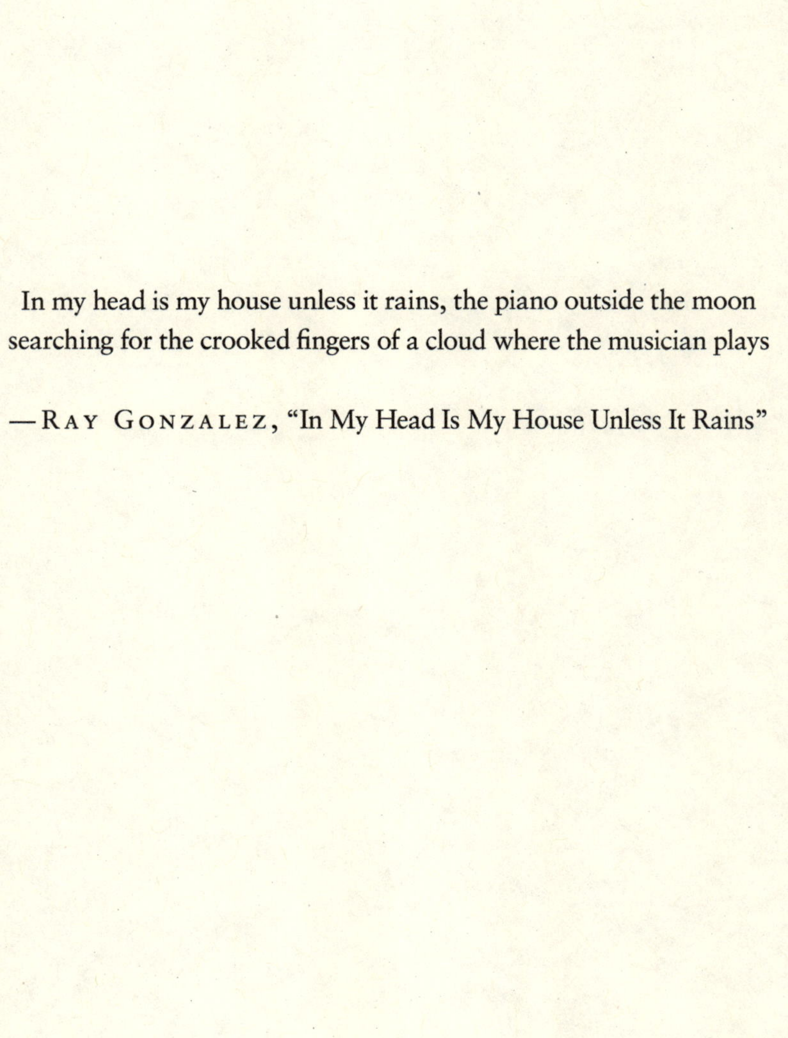

In my head is my house unless it rains, the piano outside the moon
searching for the crooked fingers of a cloud where the musician plays

—Ray Gonzalez, "In My Head Is My House Unless It Rains"

IT IS FORTUNATE THAT YOU FOUND YOUR WAY AT ALL

Into being, you arrive
        & a tiny

God becomes
        Your failures, your guardian

                Your switchbacking

                        Guts

        Mania accumulates
                Little by little

        Like the underskin
        Of others beneath
                A fingernail—

What to believe
        Is made & unmade

Depending on how heavy
        Your head beneath

The chaos of stars feels

FROM THEM I WILL LEARN TO ESCAPE THE DOOM

I press my lips into
The pee-crusted
Tiles. Outside, panic
City moans. Semis
Hiss all around me.
There are so many
Things written in
The bathroom stall
Of this gas station, so
Many things that must
Be believed: *Do*
Not do cocaine on me.
Free all political
Prisoners. Occupy
My crotch. Step by
Step, I follow
The directions but
No one—not Matilda,
Manny, or Jingle Bells—
No one answers my call
For a good time. Hot sex
Neither nubile nor manly
Shows up at 11 beneath
The overpass for some-
Thing no one has to know
About. Neither *I See Tacos*
Or *You Have a Sexy*
Face Can I Have It? I
Said thank you, why

Sure you can, it would
Be my pleasure. I go
There & crouch—
The highway beside me,
Bats above in the concrete
V. I wait & wait & wait.
Sticks of butter-colored
Cars whoosh by.
No one stops. Worry
Fills me to the very tippy
Top because time
Is of the essence
For whoever scribbled
The stall wall about
The gnome stuck
Up their ass. But no one
Shows. The sadness
I feel is not fucked out of
Me or anyone else.
No one comes. Not
The misguided & cotton-
Mouthed soul who
Thinks *No One Should*
Drink Water because
Fish Have Sex In It,
Or even *The Shit*
Elephant. I go back
To the truck stop
To see where everyone
Is & there is not a Shit
Elephant in sight. No
Shit Elephant to *Hold*
My Shit While I Do

My Shit. But I do not
Fill with anger about
The Shit Elephant. I only
Wish to hug it because
Its sorrow must be
Immense for it to lie
Like that. I am holding
The Shit Elephant tight
To me in my mind when
I see that the prophet
I search for must just have
Been here, for newly scarred
Into the stall is *Be Happy But*
Not Too Happy Because You
Will Look Like
A Creeper. I am believer
Number one & like all
The other maxims I have
Collected over the years,
I make it mine, erase it
From chipped paint
With tens of thousands
Of licks. Instantly,
The book of these hiss-
Lipped psalms that is being
Written in my belly kicks,
Rocks—one, two—a bowling
Ball cracking open & then it
Turns & turns, cartwheeling
Endlessly inside me. I am
Pregnant, being pulled apart
With these rules
For living the good life, for

The better existence that
Tomorrow I will glow with.
But that night, midnight comes
Like a rain of hammers—cupped
Hand slopping over with
Coughed-up blood & me shitting
Rabbit's foot key chains. Each
Quarter hour until the horizon
Begins to blush, the sonorous
Voice inside the radio tells me
To *Give My Dreams A Chance*,
That *I Gotta Be In It To Win*
It. That *The Only Way To Win*
Is To Play. It doesn't matter
That I swear to the sky that
I've been giving it all I have.
It is crystal clear that along
The way something must have
Gone terribly wrong—I was
Too casual about the *Smoke*
Crack that needed to get done
Before *Destroying Civilizations*.
Deep in my loins I cannot be
Sure that I truly decided between
Penis & Pepperoni Pizza or feel
The faith that underpins
You Got This, Bro. I smiled
At myself in the mirror, said
I Am Ugly & I Am Proud
A million & one times but
It must not have become
The bone-marrowed truth
I want it to be. In my short

Robe, I go out, open-armed
Onto my neighbor's lawn.
I embrace the sprinklers'
Wet chittering. The gasps
Its cold sucks out of me. Every-
Thing at the edge of the world looks
Ablaze because a huge orange
Ball I call the sun is rising
Out of the bluffs of smog.
I promise to it. I swear.
Everything we want is out
There just beyond our finger-
Tips, just waiting for our
Loving grasp. I will save
Trees by eating axes, chain-
Saws. I will stop being so
Damn useless & turn into
The most delicious burrito.
Any dumpster that sings
Its horrific breath at me
Will be my burying place.
In them I will learn to count
To hip bone, to blushed.
I will work my math
Until, every single time,
The only possible solution
To the problem posed
Is love. I will do it again,
Again & again—whatever
It takes to wake without this
Orgy of dead parrots deep-
Knotted in my chest.

PREPARING FOR THE CURE

The off-going moonglow
Turns low & down-

Ward is the night—but
This might be the most beautiful

Recess. Everyone is a giant
Rat eating their way out

Of the belly of a whale carcass
When they close their eyes.

Ghosts return to the dance,
Blowing kisses at the elderly,

Who all hunker over the salt
Lick. Hummingbirds light

The air like fireflies & each
Buzzes, whispers that all issues

Are moral issues. Our leg
Bones rattle & boom. Like

Mouths, the jacaranda snap
Open, chewing at the dark.

Unzip the flesh from the way-
Ward body. Invite the frenzy

To your deliciousness. Stand
Atop the thick ropes that litter

The ground & sing. They are
Not yet staked down. Not yet

Restraining us.

FLESH & ROCK & HUNGER

Bring on the grace
        Of knife-fighting

For kindness, grace
        Of the dash-

Board-battered face, grace
        Of the ascending,

Grace of the fire-pocked
        Piano, grace of silence

Baked in the desert,
        Grace of a consolation

Prize nestled in the trash,
        Grace of sensory

Deprivation, sensory over-
        Load, grace of barking

Dogs out there somewhere, graceful
        Favors, of borrowing

A cup of sugar—what's never
        Coming, this payback. Let us

Have it, wholly. We're opened.
        Feed us.

EVEN THE CATCLAW WILL SOMEDAY BLOOM

Night winnows toward
Sunrise, melting through

The spark-dusted hack-
Berries & in the backyard

I come to a place darker
Than black—desert-mad,

Blunt-blind with suffering
Beneath the faint pulse

Of stars. The air is rot-
Gutted & I am ghost-

Bellied. It is the dream-
Hollowing that ends me

Inked & most wanted,
Everyone's alone-in-the-mid-

Night-park nightmare. Just
Because people ask for nothing

Better than to believe the worst
Doesn't mean that the parch-

Gusts stop at flesh. Wind
Valleys our insides endlessly,

Slick cradling the hot velvet,
Breezing this blood to a boil.

DANCE DANCE DANCE

Before it's too late—neck-
Grope this life's most beautiful
Monsters until all of this disorder

Shapes sacred. Until flocks
Of balloon animals—thousands
Of them—drop from the diamond-

Blue sky. Purple hippos & clown fish.
Ticks like hubcaps & backpack-
Sized wolves. A dancer will find

A carved-in-butter replica
Of *The Garden of Earthly Delights*
Sprawling the Landing Strip's parking

Lot. Fingerprints will cloud
The windows of the downtown
Storefronts. In them some will

See angels. Others will say, *Nope.*
That there be Satan. Each sweltering
Morning, furred over the sidewalk

Like fresh snow, hibiscus. Explosions
Will be seen in the sky & letter
After letter in the paper will attempt

To explain the taste of falling.
        First—the dancer, even when
Working the pole, will appear

To be wearing garments sewn
        From moonlight. A week later
& everyone will be splendor-

Garbed. From then on, without
        Fail, each passerby will see
Their own ghost in the glass

&, freighted with the neon glow
        Of blinking ads, feel an abundance
Of life opening like a fist in their chest.

DARKENING ZOOM

Forever you
        Live half-life no-
Life the world thrilled thistly
        With a boxed-heart

Cruel down, rain
        Trapezes the puddles
For later the terrific sunglow

        Little days
        Of what little
                Meaning

        Cruel little sparks
                At dusk—
        What meanness

        The clouds doughy
                Disfigured with faces

Up the sky is lit
        Up up the sky is bright

LIFE COACH

O moral courage, O Barry
White–sized doses of human

Growth hormone. Gird your
Loins, grasshopper: Blood

Clots are branching up to
The heart of each person you

Love. In the preternatural light
Before the sun rises, every home

On your block, foggy with dream
Fumes, has, for one imperfect second

Of lightning zaps & rodent
Bites, a 50-50 chance of becoming

A mound of smoking dirt.
Your child's Easy-Bake Oven

Has been recalled. Do not
Weep. You must be strong.

A mother is leaving her two
Kids in the car. Listen up.

Feel it. Already, the temperature
Is a dozen above 100.

INTO THE DARK CIRCLE OF NOTHING THAT IS A FRESHLY DUG HOLE

How close the dirt
Kisses when face down

In an abandoned
Lot how headlights

In the street slow & pass
Slow stop & pass how each

Grinding brake whirls
Glowing eels across

The purpled vault of night
Sky how moths burst blind

In the skull how there
Are bodies inside rising

Up this failing body how
Glory glory heart attack

The thickening darkness
Fills cloudy how torn

The stained T-shirt
Stretched across the front

Door how like a mad-
Man's map of the world

That only lives in his mind
How the borders of each

Country forever creep out-
Ward how magical how now

Or always never found in the deep
Shadows bushes of red-eyed berries

Blossom out of the decaying arks
Of all the dead animals

TICK SEASON

Place of beauty
        Queens & sacrifice

Place fragrant
With impending—

        Place of oblations
        Small pleasures

In the willowy dark
Swath of stars dense

        In the neck
        Pulse of blood

Place where everything
        Has always lived

        Inside of you

FIVE

Man is, on the whole,
less good than he imagines
himself or wants to be.

—Carl Jung, *The Archetypes and the Collective Unconscious*

WHITTLING YOUR LEGS INTO A ROCKING CHAIR

If some higher power knows
What's best for us, then bring

On a monsoon of dung
Beetles, a mouthful of rats.

The truth is being alive boils
You down into a toxic mush

That our descendants will
Jaggedly smear across their lips.

Life is all about wearing sun-
Dresses that glow & Dolly

Parton wigs. Most days, my heart
Is fear-stippled & I wait for the rising

Sun, slumped in the bathtub fully
Clothed—work boots & magic

Underwear—softly clapping my hands.
When I start to feel the voltage humming

My chest into a wasp nest, I jump up,
Run through the house, clapping

Harder & pounding on doors
Because, one of these days, instead

Of just making it rain, my applause
Will slough my skin off like a moth-

Eaten bathrobe. Like a snow-
Mobile suit of inferno & love.

Because always, a tremulous thunder
Is upon us. Lightning flashes through

The knobby trees, turning
The picture window into a lung

X-ray. If I could swim through
The glass & be the rainstorm—

I might see beyond things
As they appear on TV. Music

Boxes in the drooling oaks.
Needlework faces in passing

Cars. Each day my reflection
In the downpouring glass says

The same goddamn thing—
Today is the best day of your

Life—You'll never be prettier
Than this—It's all downhill

From here. Through my ghost
In the window, I watch honey-

Comb-shaped puddles pave
The street with shards of the sky.

HERE THERE BE MONSTERS

The new normal is
An illperfect confusion—

Wishbones slipped
In for spines—

Beatless hearts & the combustible
Dark beats down

No better wishes, no coal-mined
Bones whispering
Sweet mushings

In the syrupy air—

Peoplemash, tender
Drool, pulverized honeys

Celebrate this
O rage-blind our eyes

SHIT IS ALWAYS ABOUT TO GO DOWN

O the beautiful
Gossip
A body's jangling wheeze—

Yawps in
The bone cage

I said I said
You are like you
Are like you, you, you—

Nobody different, no body, no

An hour of steady pressure
Applied to the wound
& the wound becomes
Celebratory, knotted—

The chest opens

Hungrily—

Everyone loses
Always but there's
A prize!

The broken
Spot you kissed

Me again & again & again

THE TIMING COULDN'T BE BETTER

The hours clink by,
A janitor thumbing
Through an enormous hoop
Of keys. The trees
Blackened & bare,
Are empty of leaves
After an overnight
Cold snap. I want to
Believe in everything
You do but there's so
Little good air in
The world. In my chest,
A valley folds in
On itself. When I
Close my eyes & spin
In circles I fall down
But I don't learn
Anything anymore.
Something underpins
The day, holds the blinking
Light up like the bones
Inside us. But what it is
Is just out of reach.
Each morning I take
Pictures in the mirror
But at dusk when I look
At the photos I can't
Recognize my own face.

SLITHER & DAZZLE

Deep the woods churn & a maple
        Leaf under my tongue

        In the thick
Spiraling I listen
                So deep
In the woods
        Dark trembling deep

        White ants in
                The deer-shadowed
        Thickets

Shoe polish black the bottomless
        Sky, I fall
                Into it

        Like a mirror I can't see
                Myself in

The crowing grove is roiling
        Deep the grave blanket

The snow wasps whirling
        Like I am not
                Even here

SPONSOR THIS GORILLA

Oh patchiest beard of blood
& lips bee-stung & beautiful,
Night tonight is a constellation
Of booming & night tomorrow
Might be zombie dancing beneath
The magnolias—butterscotch
& dungeon sweat & a confusion
Of mosquitos in the air. But how
Sad our staggering is, how easy it
Is to see how profoundly busted
Up we are in the daylight: Flesh
Heaps of urinal-toothed voids with legs
We will do everything in our power
Not to use to cross the bridge
Under the bleaching sun, the bridge
That one of these days will collapse.
How easy it is to go on without
Thinking about the end. To practice
The beauty-queen wave, a golf
Clap. But I like to scratch until
The skin rivers with blood, for
The welling—wasp sting, bottom
Sinking, knife bite—& then it is
So long, British Petroleum, you deepwater
Bullshit producers, goodbye, Ogallala—
Sooner rather than later we will
Have no problem whittling
A friend's skull into a mug for just
A half cup of water. Our only
Renewable resource is our

Unlimited supply of ugly. The easy
Cruelty generated when we
Breathe. We are so afraid because
There have been reports & warnings,
Alerts & rumors & this one guy told
This girl who told me that you look
Like a pretty good drug mule & you
Right there, guns, ammo & more
Ammo & don't think this is fear
Mongering but the threat level is
Casket & it is time to shit your
Pants, but there is little else that
You need to know. All you need
Is this here roll of duct tape. Steel
Yourself for the upcoming beatings.
Bar your doors & layer tape on
Everything—cover the kitchen windows,
Seal every door, your mouth & eyes,
Mummify the cat so, like a football, so you
Can carry it in case of an emergency.
While all this palpitating time, right
There, just under the surface, just
Behind the ribs, the perfect song
Is always playing: it is sad, tender
As a ripple's slow unfolding across
The glassy face of a lake. Two fingertips
Dipped softly. The slipping in, together,
Of two pressing bodies. There is
A vital rocking in the bones, a murmuring
That, if you listen close, presses
A palm like an iron against a chest.
Then hold your breath, whisper
About us, the beastly beasts, queen

Of the dead bolt, king of cowering
Behind the curtains when someone
Knocks at the door. So before we
Are all living on the delectable crunch
Of sand & bugs, chap-lipped
In the desert, shave me with your most
Rusted blade & tattoo your name
Across my back—*Thug Life. Pug Life.*
No one's having fun life. It is so simple—
Each one of us makes dirt, just like
God & the worms. We are nothing,
More or less, than walking mulch piles.
I'll do whatever I can to help you
Hurry up—hand me your talking
Walleye, your disaster-preparedness
Space suit, your remote that can control
That other remote & even turn children
Into orchids. While you do whatever you
Need to do to get ready, watch me smile.
I will pimp your every gadget & sex tape
DVD. I dice. I slice. I'll tear my own heart
Out & make it instantly stop beating just
By staring at it. I will take a chamber-
Sized bite out of it, loll it on my tongue
Before gulping it down like a goldfish
You can think of no other way to save
From the apartment inferno you are
Standing in the middle of. Out front
In the street, I will heave & gag until
I throw up not just that chunk of heart
But a diamond crown, a golf club laden
With both irons & woods & on the soft
Carpet of grass beside the sidewalk, one

Whole, fully alive & blinking manatee.
I will be brought to you by the moon,
The star's dying light, that itch you can't
Scratch, a rash in the shape of the dream
You won't confess to even to yourself, a canoe
Stacked high with Egg McMuffins & Cheesy
Poofs & one smashed-to-hell cell phone
On a pontoon slathered in K-Y Jelly & also
The water wings soaked in napalm. Headphones.
Wireless handsets. Doormen fired because
They don't have hands. I will be underwritten.
Backed with or without bones & an atlas
With no time for spelling bee bullshit
My shoulders will burl a cosmos of purposefully
Misspelled products for your enjoyment—La-Z-
Boys & Lite-Brite-stuffed Luvs, Santa satchels
Spilling with Laffy Taffy & bulletproof
Undergarments woven from Pixy Stix.
Through its sadness, that untethered, floating
Into deep space astronaut dog will be able
To see the glittering banners, the flashing
Lights that, right here, will squeeze tears
From both the Cabbage Patch Kids
Boxed up in the attic & the bodiless ones
Kicked into ditches. Blood will fishhook
From the eyecorners, the heartpoint-shaped
Flesh of anyone who really tries to look,
To see & lowing half-blind into the dark,
No one will ever ever ever be able
To tell that I've been darted a good dozen
Times already & it just don't take.

STAYLIGHT

Each instant brings the leaving, the go
Far, a lowering & gone. Even, as it darkens,
A leavening, the broken-down little,
The hackwards bellow. Tomorrow,
Let me wake into it again. Into here.
Let me be that little. Let me be
That little more & then more & then
A little too much & on fire. Let me be
Overfilling & full & overspilling.
My being never & never alone
& at all instants, wandering the dark
Woods, listening to the wayward snaps
& how the slightest slant of light
Through the sugar maples sings or even
How a yellow shirt seems to yawn
& grow, slowly glowing with the first
Dots of an afternoon sprinkle.
The shine of wet grass. A fist
Of light opening. Let me be limbs
Slick black. Let me go into the bee-
Stinging brightness of stopping so
Fast I come face-to-face with myself
Stopped in the becoming light of what is
More often than just now & then. Let me
Be here. Let me goodbye. Let me live
In the soft tissue that cradles our
Insides. Lungbutter. Heartjelly.
Let me think. Let me know how
Many fingers I am holding up to the sun.
Let me be here my hand is shading

My eyes. Let me be the rain just barely.
The rain glistening your lip. Here,
Let me be why the hell not, clouds
Opening to an almost unbearable brightness
That is *it*, that is joyously now, even
While I know *know* that in a few
Moments the billowing up there will fall
Out of itself & it won't stop raining
For days. So this, just for a bit now,
Is light. Is life spinning unplanned & with-
Out bottom, the decade tucked into
A moment like the dictionary pressed
Between two dead butterflies for years,
Until the day all of language was more
Flat than illuminated skin peeled off
A blister. Let me be & then let it. Let, let,
Me & then it & then make it a floodwork
Of letting, a bath that does not cool & then
Let blood in the bath, red nailheads that blossom
Bloodshot scarves through the water.
Plumbed down in the bloodbath let me be
Not the becoming light, but let that shining
Warm my face with the hot gust of an oven
Door opened to check the rising, that slow
Rising of light over a birdbath, finch-filled,
Hopping jubilant. The light is a bruise fading
Backward to before its happening, before even
The idea of wound, of hurt & a love-letting
Becomes large in the spreading blaze. Let
Somehow, all of us apparitions, press in
Beneath that light that pallets through
The live oak's haggard limb stretch. See-
Through & thin as cellophane, all us ghosts

Collect, crowd close, a deck of cards, a roll
Of pennies unwrapped but holding together,
A wall of firewood, close as blades of grass,
Of salt water. Let all us ghosts pile on
Top & melt together, weld, in that becoming
Light. Let all of us be endlessly beautiful in that
Lanterning. The sap-letting, that gnarled bark.
Leaves helicoptering in the pluming
Brightness as suddenly, it folds, becoming
The exact letting light that glows through
Everything you love at the very end.

Acknowledgments

Big thanks to the editors of the following publications where some of these poems appeared, sometimes under different names:

American Poetry Review, Badlands, Bear Review, burntdistrict, Crazyhorse, Colorado Review, Copper Nickel, The Frank Martin Review, Gigantic Sequins, Handsome, The Literary Review, Laurel Review, The Pinch, Ploughshares, Profane, Redivider, Revolver Literary Magazine, San Pedro River Review, Smartish Pace, South Dakota Review, Typo Magazine, & *Zone 3.*

Thanks to:

Academy of American Poets' *Poem-a-Day* for publishing "All Us Beautiful Monsters."

Typo Magazine & Adam Clay & Matt Henriksen for publishing "Tick Season" as a limited edition broadside.

TCU Press & Dan Williams for publishing "Recess" as a limited edition broadside.

Verse Daily for republishing "Om Nom."

Alex Lemon is the author of six poetry collections and two memoirs—most recently *Another Last Day* and *Feverland: A Memoir in Shards*. He lives with his family in Fort Worth, Texas, and teaches at TCU.

Founded as a nonprofit organization in 1980, Milkweed Editions is an independent publisher. Our mission is to identify, nurture, and publish transformative literature, and build an engaged community around it.

We are based in Bde Óta Othúŋwe (Minneapolis) in Mní Sota Makhóčhe (Minnesota), the traditional homeland of the Dakhóta and Anishinaabe (Ojibwe) people and current home to many thousands of Dakhóta, Ojibwe, and other Indigenous people, including four federally recognized Dakhóta nations and seven federally recognized Ojibwe nations.

We believe all flourishing is mutual, and we envision a future in which all can thrive. Realizing such a vision requires reflection on historical legacies and engagement with current realities. We humbly encourage readers to do the same.

milkweed.org

Milkweed Editions, an independent nonprofit literary publisher, gratefully acknowledges sustaining support from our board of directors, the McKnight Foundation, the National Endowment for the Arts, and many generous contributions from foundations, corporations, and thousands of individuals—our readers. This activity is made possible by the voters of Minnesota through a Minnesota State Arts Board Operating Support grant, thanks to a legislative appropriation from the Arts and Cultural Heritage Fund.

Interior design by Mike Corrao
Typeset in Sabon Pro

Sabon is an old-style serif originally designed in the early twentieth century by Jan Tschichold. He created the Garamond-inspired type for a group of German printers who sought a typeface that would look the same no matter which of their machines it was printed on.

Milkweed Editions is committed to ecological stewardship. We strive to align our operations accordingly and to reduce their environmental impact. We are a member of the Green Press Initiative, a nonprofit coalition of publishers, manufacturers, and authors working to protect the world's endangered forests and conserve natural resources. *All Us Beautiful Monsters* was printed on acid-free 100% postconsumer-waste paper by Friesens Corporation.